Ladybird Readers

The Fair

Series Editor: Sorrel Pitts
Text adapted by Coleen Degnan-Veness

LADYBIRD BOOKS

UK | USA | Canada | Ireland | Australia
India | New Zealand | South Africa

Ladybird Books is part of the Penguin Random House group of companies
whose addresses can be found at global.penguinrandomhouse.com.
www.penguin.co.uk   www.puffin.co.uk   www.ladybird.co.uk

Text adapted from 'Peppa Pig: Fun at the Fair', first published by Ladybird Books, 2011
This version first published by Ladybird Books, 2017
003

Licensed by

Printed in China

The authorized representative in the EEA is Penguin Random House Ireland,
Morrison Chambers, 32 Nassau Street, Dublin D02 YH68

A CIP catalogue record for this book is available from the British Library

ISBN: 978–0–241–28357–8

All correspondence to:
Ladybird Books
Penguin Random House Children's
One Embassy Gardens, 8 Viaduct Gardens, London SW11 7BW

MIX
Paper from
responsible sources
FSC® C018179
www.fsc.org

The Fair

Based on the Peppa Pig
TV series

Picture words

Peppa

Mommy Pig

bow

arrow

Daddy Pig

George

big wheel

slide

stall

panda

duck

fair

Peppa, George, Mommy Pig, and Daddy Pig are at the fair.

Peppa's friends are at the fair, too.

Peppa and Mommy Pig
go to the duck stall.

"I love that panda,"
says Peppa.

"I have got a duck!" says Mommy Pig. "Now, you can have the panda."

"Great!" says Peppa.

George likes going on the big slide.

"Okay, George," says Daddy Pig. "Let's go!"

13

George loves the slide.

But the slide is too big
for Daddy Pig.

"I do not like this slide,"
he says.

Peppa and Mommy Pig go to the bow and arrow stall.

Mommy Pig gets a panda for Peppa.

"Now, I have got two pandas!" says Peppa.

George likes going on the big wheel.

"Okay, George," says Daddy Pig. "Let's go!"

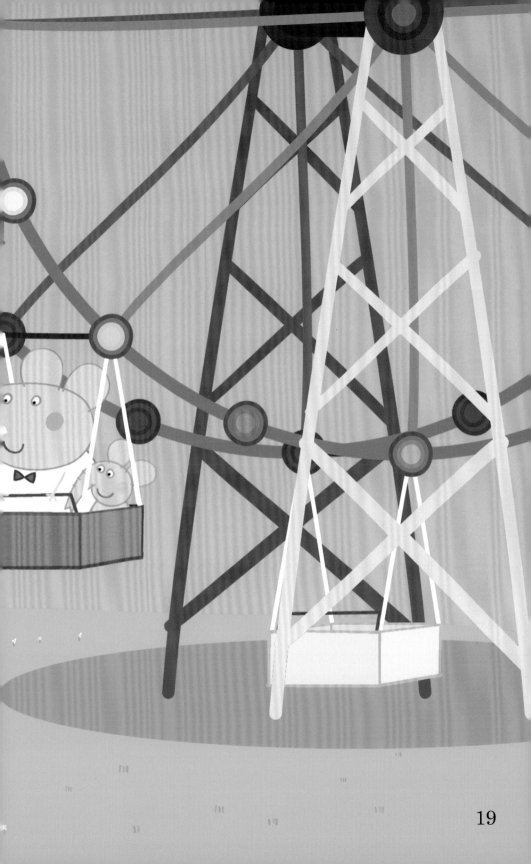

George loves the big wheel.

But the wheel is too big for Daddy Pig!

"I do not like this big wheel," he says.

George and Daddy Pig
see Peppa and Mommy
Pig at a stall.

"Can you get a panda for
me here, too, please?"
asks Peppa.

Mommy Pig gets lots of pandas at the fair for Peppa.

"Well done, Mommy!" says Peppa.

Peppa gives the pandas to her friends.

"Great!" say Peppa and her friends. "We love fairs!"

Activities

The key below describes the skills practiced in each activity.

⬤ Spelling and writing

⬤ Reading

⬤ Speaking

⬤ Critical thinking

⬤ Preparation for the Cambridge Young Learners Exams

1 Look and read. Put a ✓ or a ✗ in the boxes. 📖 ⬡

1 This is Peppa.

2  This is Daddy Pig.

3 This is George.

4 This is a panda.

5  This is a slide.

2 **Look and read. Write *yes* or *no*.**

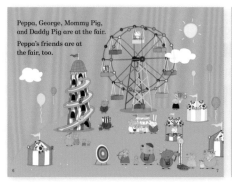

1 Peppa and George are at the fair.   yes

2 Mommy Pig and Daddy Pig are at the fair.

3 Peppa's friends are not at the fair.

4 Peppa and Mommy Pig go to the duck stall.

5 "I love that big duck," says Peppa.

3 Look at the letters. Write the words.

1 (m o y m M) (i g P)

M o m m y   P i g

2 (k c s u d)

3  (n a p d a)

4 (r i f a)

5 (l l s a t)

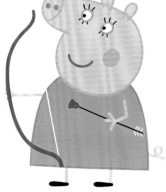

4 Talk about the picture with a friend.
What can you see at the fair?
Use the words in the box.

stall	George	big wheel	slide
Mommy Pig	Daddy Pig	Peppa	

I can see a big wheel.

5 Circle the correct sentences.

1

a "I have got a duck!" says Mommy Pig.

b "I have got a duck!" says Peppa.

2

a George likes going on the big slide.

b Daddy Pig likes going on the big slide.

3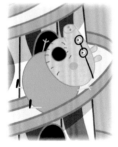

a "I do not like this slide," says Mommy Pig.

b "I do not like this slide," says Daddy Pig.

4

a Mommy Pig goes on the big wheel.

b Mommy Pig goes to the bow and arrow stall.

6 **Read the questions. Write answers using the words in the box.** 📖 ✏️

> fair   Daddy Pig   panda
>
> slide   stall

George loves the slide.

But the slide is too big for Daddy Pig.

"I do not like this slide," he says.

14   15

1 Where is George?

At the _____ fair _____.

2 What does George love?

The _____.

Peppa and Mommy Pig go to the bow and arrow stall.

Mommy Pig gets a panda for Peppa.

"Now, I have got two pandas!" says Peppa.

3 Who is the slide too big for?

_____.

4 Where are Peppa and Mommy Pig?

At the bow and arrow _____.

5 What does Mommy Pig get?

A _____.

7 **Ask and answer the questions with a friend.** 💬 ❓

1 Has Peppa got a bow and arrow?

No, she hasn't.

2 Who has got a bow and arrow?

3 Who wants a panda?

4 Why does she want a panda?

5 Is Peppa happy?

8 **Circle the correct words.**

1  **a** slide **b** stall

2 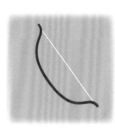 **a** bow **b** duck

3  **a** panda **b** arrow

4  **a** big wheel **b** slide

5  **a** panda **b** pandas

9 Write *T* (true) or *F* (false).

George loves the slide.
But the slide is too big for Daddy Pig.
"I do not like this slide," he says.

Peppa and Mommy Pig go to the bow and arrow stall.
Mommy Pig gets a panda for Peppa.

"Now, I have got two pandas!" says Peppa.

1 Daddy Pig likes the slide. ....F........

2 The slide is too small
for Daddy Pig. ....

3 Peppa does not like pandas. ....

4 Mommy Pig wants
a panda for Peppa. ....

5 Now, Peppa has got
two pandas. ....

10 **Match the two parts of the sentences.**

1 Mommy Pig gets

2 George and Daddy Pig see

3 Peppa gives pandas

4 "We love fairs!"

a to her friends.

b Peppa and Mommy Pig at a stall.

c lots of pandas at the fair.

d say Peppa and her friends.

11 Look at the picture. Put a ✓ or a X in the boxes.

1 Can you see a big wheel? ✓

2 Can you see a bow and arrow?

3 Can you see ten pandas?

4 Can you see Daddy Pig?

5 Can you see a slide?

12 **Order the story. Write 1—5.**

.... Peppa and Mommy Pig go to the duck stall.

.... George and Daddy Pig go on the big wheel.

.... George and Daddy Pig go on the slide.

.... Peppa and Mommy Pig go to the bow and arrow stall.

...1... Peppa, George, Mommy Pig, and Daddy Pig are at the fair.

13 **Write the correct questions.** 📖 ✏️

is (Where) (Peppa) (?)

1 ___Where is Peppa?___

(at) (Is) (George) (the) (fair) (?)

2 _____

(Does) (panda) (want) (Peppa) (a) (?)

3 _____

(like) (Does) (the) (slide) (George) (?)

4 _____

(big) (Daddy Pig) (Is) (too) (?) (the)

(for) (slide)

5 _____

14 Ask and answer *Where are?* questions with a friend. O

1 *Where are Peppa and Mommy Pig?*

They are at the duck stall.

2 Where are George and Daddy Pig?

3 Where are Peppa and Mommy Pig?

4 Where are George and Daddy Pig?

15 **Circle the correct words.**

1 (**Who**)/ **When** is at the fair?

2 **What / Where** does George love?

3 **Is / Are** Peppa with Mommy Pig?

4 **What / Who** gets lots of pandas at the fair?

5 **Is / Are** there pandas for Peppa's friends?

16 Find the words. 📖

fair   stall   panda
slide   big wheel

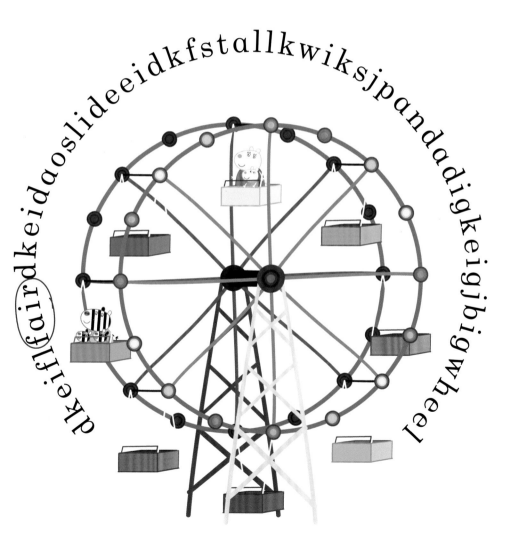

17 **Look at the picture and read the questions. Write the answers.**

1 Has Peppa got a panda?

Yes, she has.

2 Are Peppa's friends at the fair?

3 Are there twelve pandas in the picture?

18 **Talk to a friend about fairs.**

1

Do you like fairs?

Yes, I do.

2 Do you like slides? Why? / Why not?

3 Do you like big wheels?
Why? / Why not?

4 Do you like pandas?
Why? / Why not?

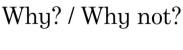

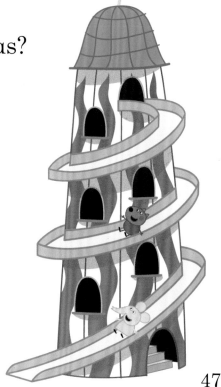

Level 1

Anansi Helps a Friend
978–0–241–25409–7

Cinderella
978–0–241–25407–3

The Enormous Turnip
978–0–241–25408–0

On the Farm
978–0–241–25413–4

Cars
978–0–241–28354–7

Jon's Football Team
978–0–241–25411–0

The Magic Porridge Pot
978–0–241–25406–6

In the Garden
978–0–241–26220–7

Fun with Old Things
978–0–241–26219–1

Fairy Friends
978–0–241–28351–6

Peter Rabbit Goes to the Island
978–0–241–25415–8

Topsy and Tim Go to the Zoo
978–0–241–25414–1

Topsy and Tim Go to the Farm
978–0–241–28355–4

The Fair
978–0–241–28357–8

Daddy Pig's Old Chair
978–0–241–28356–1

Now you're ready for Level 2!